How to Eat an Artichoke

How to Eat an Artichoke and Other Trying, Troublesome, Hard-to-Get-at Foods

by Rochelle Udell

G. P. PUTNAM'S SONS
NEW YORK

Library of Congress Cataloging in Publication Data

Udell, Rochelle.
How to eat an artichoke
and other trying, troublesome, hard-to-get-at foods.

1. Table etiquette. 2. Food. I. Title.
BJ2041.U33 1981   395'.54   81-12011
ISBN 0-399-12677-5   AACR2

Illustrated by Marilyn Schaffer
Designed by Doug Turshen

PRINTED IN THE UNITED STATES OF AMERICA

For my mother

How to Eat an Artichoke

INTRODUCTION

The last thing we knew, it was 1971, and our idea of a dinner party was everybody sitting around, drinking wine out of peanut butter glasses and eating with our hands. Now, all of a sudden, it's the eighties, formal entertaining's back, and table smarts are a must.

Faced with the problem of publicly confronting an artichoke, for instance, the insecure diner might well decline, pleading an allergic reaction, or instead, he or she might decide to learn to do it right. It is to this latter, worthy person that I dedicate *How to Eat an Artichoke.*

It is my fervent belief that etiquette shyness restricts the lives of too many people, that, out of fear of embarrassment, a lot of us are missing out on a lot of pleasure. And that's too bad, because comfort is the reason for manners, and it's hard to make a good impression or have fun when you're tense and self-conscious. This little volume, then, is not a cookbook, but rather a guide to how to lead a fuller, richer life by getting the maximum benefits from social security.

CONTENTS

FOR STARTERS
How to Open with Aces

ARTICHOKES

Choked up by the prospect of attacking this devilish veggie? At last, help is at hand!

This "edible thistle" comes stuffed or plain, accompanied with hot drawn lemon butter, hollandaise, mayonnaise or vinaigrette. Tear off a leaf from the cooked, presented artichoke with your fingertips and pull it through your teeth to remove the edible pulp. The part closest to the base is put into your mouth. If it is accompanied by lemon butter or vinaigrette, the edible end is dipped and quickly brought to your mouth. With a thicker dip the edible end is handled like a corn chip. If the artichoke is stuffed, peel a leaf off and, using a knife, spread the stuffing onto the leaf to enjoy.

When you reach the thinner, inner leaves, discard them; they are not edible. Hold the bottom of the artichoke down with a fork and use your hand to pull them off. This reveals a hairy center. Do *not* eat this. Cut it out and you are left with the favored artichoke bottom, or "heart," which can be cut and dipped in whatever accompanies your artichoke or eaten plain.

15

CAVIAR

At these prices, who'd risk wasting a drop? But not to be intimidated. With a little care, you'll look like a Romanov.

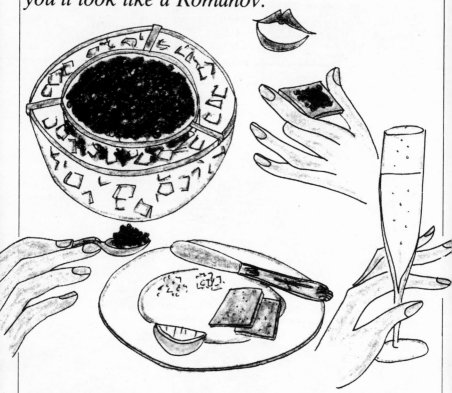

If caviar is passed to you in a bowl or crock with its own spoon, serve a teaspoonful onto your plate. As they are passed, take, with their individual serving spoons, small amounts of minced onion and sieved egg whites and yolks, as well as a few lemon slices and a couple of pieces of toast. Assemble the canapé to taste with your knife, then use your hand to lift it to your mouth.

If you're at a cocktail party or reception, where the already prepared canapés are being passed on trays, you simply lift one off the plate and pop it into your mouth.

C HEESE

Want to be a cheese whiz?
Here's all you need to know.

As an hors d'oeuvre—cheese is spread on a cracker with
the knife that accompanies each kind.

CHEESE

When it is served with a salad—you can spread it on a cracker or a small bit of bread with either a fork or knife, or a piece of cheese may be broken off with a fork on your plate and eaten with lettuce. Soft, running cheese, such as Brie and Camembert, are always spread with a salad knife or butter knife.

Dessert cheese served with fruit is easily handled. Just quarter, core and/or pare apples or ripe pears—then eat the cheese with a fork and the fruit with either a fork or fingers. Alternate fruit and cheese.

PÂTÉ

Look at it as an elegant meatloaf, or fancy bologna, and relax.

Pâté may appear either before dinner or with the salad during a meal. If it is served to you with cocktails, spread it thickly on small pieces of toast or cracker, and eat with your hand. If it accompanies the salad course, it may be passed in a crock or in a ring mold. In that case, lift off a slice or serve yourself a spoonful on your plate along with a cracker or toast. Prepare the small open sandwich with a knife, then lift with your hand to your mouth. Cornichon pickles (small gherkins) are often served with *pâté* and should be eaten with a fork.

S OUPS

Sorry that you didn't listen when your mother tried to teach you? Don't fret, all is not lost, if you follow these basic rules.

Soup may be served either in a soup plate or cup, depending on the type of soup and the formality of the meal.

Clear soups are often served in small, double-handled consommé cups. You can test the heat of the soup with a spoon, then lift the cup to drink it. Any vegetables or noodles left at the bottom can be eaten with a spoon. A two-handled cream soup bowl is larger than a consommé cup. You can drink the soup or use a spoon. In both cases, when you are finished, place the spoon on the plate underneath and to the right of the cup. Never leave it standing in the cup.

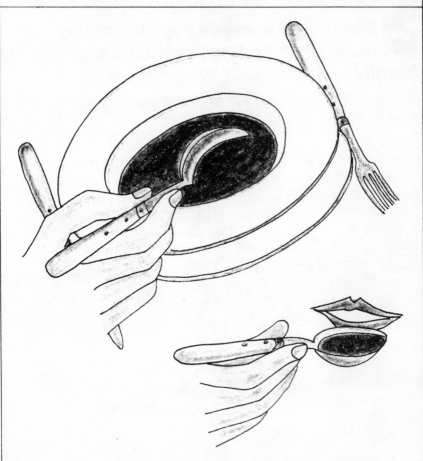

When a soup plate is used, always spoon away from the table's edge. When you reach the bottom, you can tilt the plate slightly away from you. When using a soup spoon, always sip from the side and never put the entire bowl of the spoon into your mouth.

Tiny crackers or croutons can be added to soup, whole, a few at a time. Larger crackers should be eaten separately except with hearty soups like chowders at informal meals, when you can add a few pieces at a time.

At all times, drink soups quietly.

SHRIMP COCKTAIL

How could something so little be this much trouble? You're about to see that it really isn't.

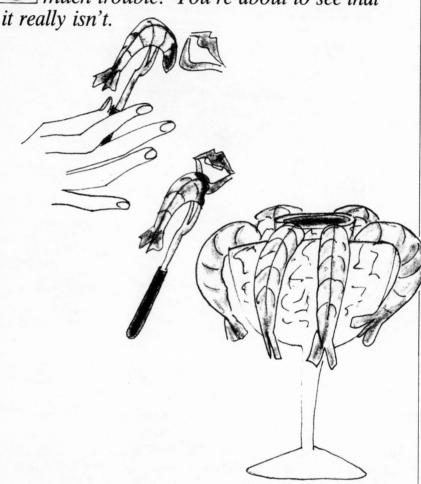

If oversized shrimp are served in a stemmed glass, pick them up with an oyster fork and bite off a mouthful at a time, dipping into the sauce before each bite. It is too precarious to cut shrimp in this kind of dish. If large shrimp are served on a flat dinner plate, they can be cut with a knife and fork.

THE SHELL GAME
Full Disclosure with Composure

CLAMS, OYSTERS AND MUSSELS

Here's a sure cure for shell-shock!

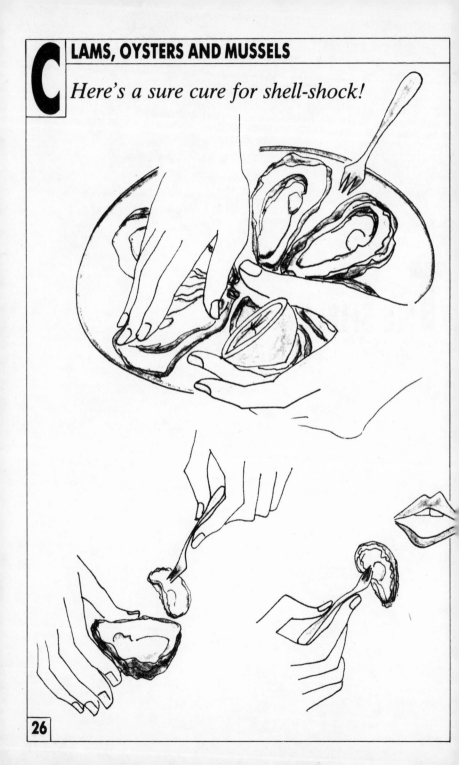

For clams and oysters, served raw on the half shell, begin by squeezing lemon juice (hand over wedge or slice to prevent squirting) on the clam or oyster—not on the sauce. Steady the shell against the plate with your free hand and extract the clam or oyster with a small shellfish fork. You may dip it into your own sauce container (formally, clams and oysters are served only with lemon) and then lift the meat whole into your mouth. Horseradish and cocktail sauce can also be dabbed on to the individual clam or oyster; it is then lifted to the mouth completely dressed. Never cut a raw clam or oyster. Only in an informal setting can you drain the juice from the shell into your mouth. Do it as unobtrusively as possible. There are two schools of thought about oyster crackers—to drop or not to drop them into the sauce and retrieve with a fork. Taste dictates.

For steamed clams (or steamed mussels), lift the fully opened pair of shells (if shell does not open—do not eat it). Separate the clam by pulling it out by its neck. Discard the neck sheath and, holding it by the neck, dip it first into a cup of broth and then into melted butter and eat it in one bite—the neck can be eaten. Pile all the empty shells on a second plate. You may choose to drink the cup of broth.

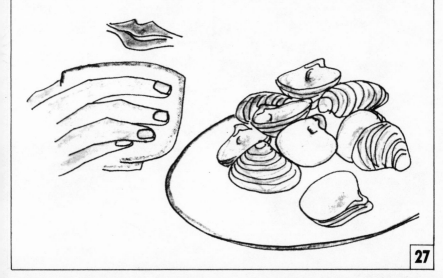

CLAMS, OYSTERS AND MUSSELS

For mussels (like *moules marinière*) cooked in a souplike sauce, lift them and extract the mussel from its shell with a seafood fork; or you can eat it right from the half shell along with its juice. The extra sauce can be sopped up with fork-speared bread or eaten with a spoon as a soup.

Fried clams, oysters, scallops or shrimps can be cut with a fork and eaten.

Fantail shrimp (fried Oriental style) can be lifted by the tail in the hand, dipped into a sauce and then eaten, but leave the tail.

C RAB

Leave the crabbiness to the food on your plate, as you ease blithely through some genuinely simple procedures.

Break one crab leg from the body, then crack it into sections with a nutcracker. Remove the meat with a seafood fork or a nutpick, then dip it into melted butter or a mayonnaise sauce.

With hard-shelled crabs, first pull the legs from the body with your fingers and then suck out the meat as noiselessly as possible. The remainder of the body can then be turned on its back and the meat picked out with a fork or pick.

Crab claws served as hors d'oeuvres are to be picked up by the shell with your fingers, dipped in sauce, and sucked out.

Soft-shelled crabs are meant to be eaten in their entirety, both crab and shell, with a knife and fork.

EGGS

That classic baffler, the soft-boiled egg—solved at last!

A soft-boiled egg may appear at the table in an egg-cup, or may even come covered with a "cozy" to keep it warm. Remove the "cozy," then with a knife, crack the egg horizontally across the smallish end until it comes loose as you steady the cup against the plate with your other hand. Lift off the top, place it on a saucer, season the remaining contents and eat with a spoon.

LOBSTER

A tough case to crack? Not if you're armed with these few invaluable clues.

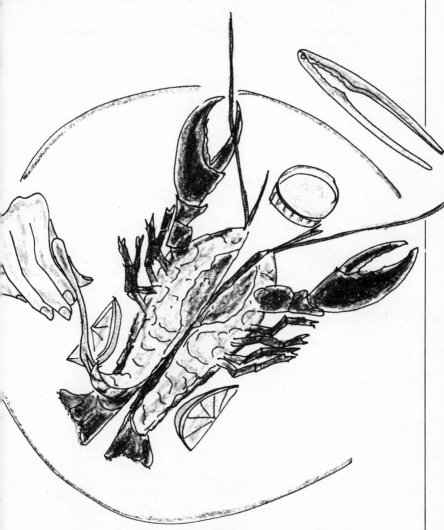

Put on a lobster bib or subtly tuck a napkin into your neckline. With your hand, twist off the lobster's big claws from its body. Use a nutcracker to open the claw, then

LOBSTER

remove the meat with a pick or lobster fork, dip it in sauce (melted butter for a hot broiled or boiled lobster, or mayonnaise for a cold one). Next, break the tail away from the body. If the tail has been previously split, the meat can be easily removed, and if it hasn't been split, just break off the little flaps and push through to get out the meat in one piece. Cut this meat with a knife and fork, dip and eat. The legs are then twisted off with your hands and the meat is sucked out. Finally, the tomallery (green liver) of a male lobster can be eaten, as can the coral (roe) of the female.

PATTY SHELL FOOD

Venus only had a halfshell to worry about! But you can finesse this one with ease.

When serving yourself anything in a patty shell, lift up to your mouth a piece of the shell in combination with its filling. The patty shell can be cut with your fork. This will be a bit messy; accept it. Use your knife to buttress the shell and push the filling onto your fork.

S NAILS

What "moles" are to espionage, snails are to food—devilishly hard to get hold of.

The first thing to remember if you want to flush out a snail is to set your own pace. Snails are served with a pair of snail tongs that grip the hot snail shell so that you can extract the snail whole from the shell with a snail or oyster fork. If the tongs are not provided, grip the hot snail shell with the edge of your napkin. When the shells have cooled a bit, you may lift them in your hand, tilt them into your mouth and enjoy the garlic butter and juice. I prefer to use the speared-piece-of-bread method to get all the juice.

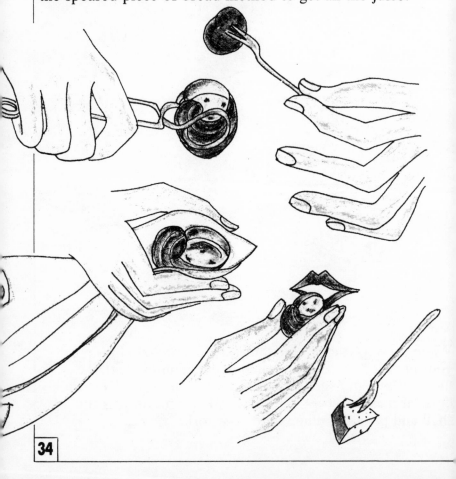

THINGS WITH BONES

Dissecting Dinner
with Class and Technique

BIRDS

Avoid fowl play while dining with this foolproof game plan.

Cut off the wings and legs of a Cornish hen, quail, pigeon or squab, then eat the body of the bird or birds with a knife and fork. Never pick up the body, although you can lift the wings and legs with one hand and carry them to your mouth.

C HICKEN

The things that Frank Perdue never told you!

Still, this system should meet most contingencies. Start with half a chicken, separate the leg and wing at their joints with a knife and fork. Then with the fork stabilize the leg or breast or wing. Slice pieces of meat into manageable amounts. Cut only two or three pieces at a time. If the situation is formal, leave whatever cannot be picked up with a knife and fork on your plate. If the situation is less formal, you may pick up small bones with your fingers—but try to use one hand only.

Never pick up a carcass. Follow the same procedure with small birds, and if the situation is formal follow the hostess's lead for picking up bones. Be aware of grease on your mouth as well as your hand and use your napkin to blot when you need to.

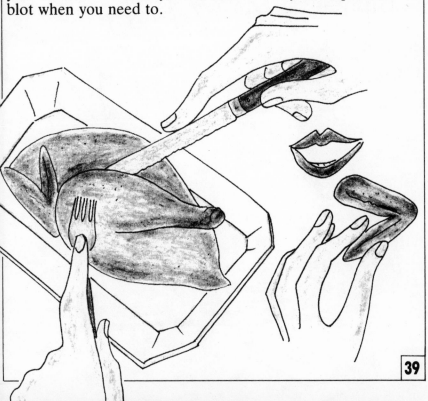

C HOPS

Dressed to kill or stark naked, chops can be trouble, but they don't have to be.

Cut into center or "eye" of a veal, pork or lamb chop with a fork and sharp knife. If the chop is wearing a "panty" or frilled skirt, you can use it to grip the bone without soiling your fingers as you cut away the meat near the bone. In formal or restaurant situations, never pick up a bone and gnaw at it, even if it's wearing a "panty." These frills are only a decoration, not a license for gluttony. In an informal context, on the other hand, go ahead and have a ball, but only if the bones are free of gravy.

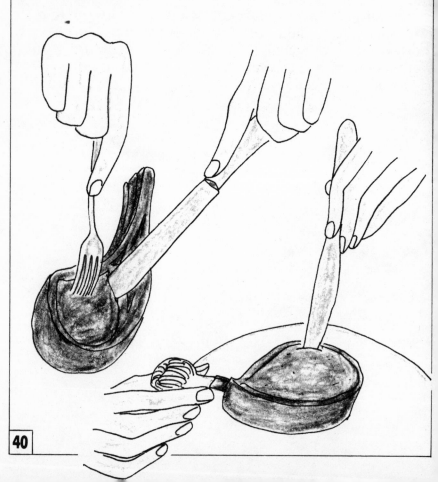

FISH

Always remember, it's easier to eat a fish than to catch one, especially with a little prior instruction.

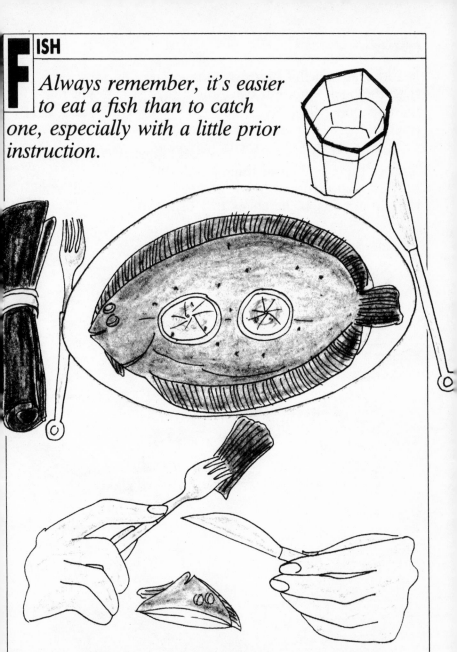

First cut off the head and tail of the fish with a knife and fork and move them to the side of the plate. Insert the top of the knife against the backbone and slit the fish from

head to tail. At this point, you have three options: one—
slide the backbone out; two—open the fish flat and remove
the backbone; three—lift the top filet off, eat it, and then
remove the backbone.

If you get caught with any small bones in your mouth,
remove them with your thumb and forefinger.

Fish aficionados will eat the head of a small fish. And it
is an honor to eat the cheek of a fish.

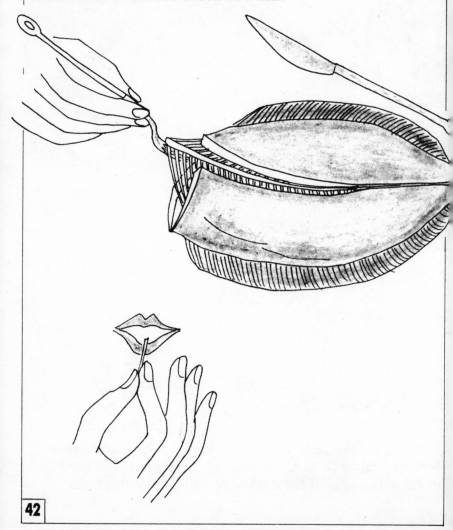

FROGS' LEGS

No reason to get jumpy!

Frogs' legs are eaten with your fingers, although large ones can be disjointed with a knife and fork before they are picked up.

TRICKY VEGETABLES
A Fresh Approach to an Old Problem

A SPARAGUS

A spring without asparagus is like a day without sunlight. Depriving yourself of this superlative vegetable is missing one of life's great pleasures.

If asparagus are served already sauced—eat them with a fork and knife by cutting them into manageable pieces. If they are to be dipped in a sauce and are large—cut the tips to avoid any dripping and dropping. You may pick up the stalks by hand, then dip and eat up to the tough part. They may be entirely manageable by hand, in which case you can pick up the whole asparagus, dip and eat.

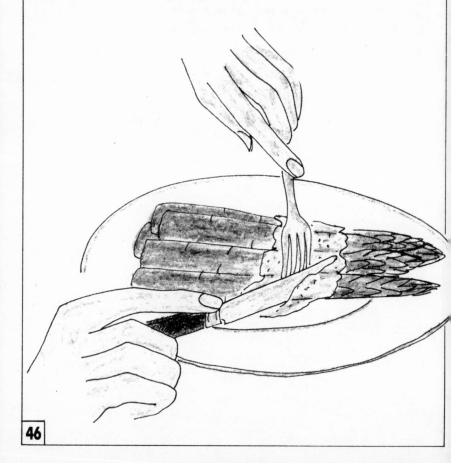

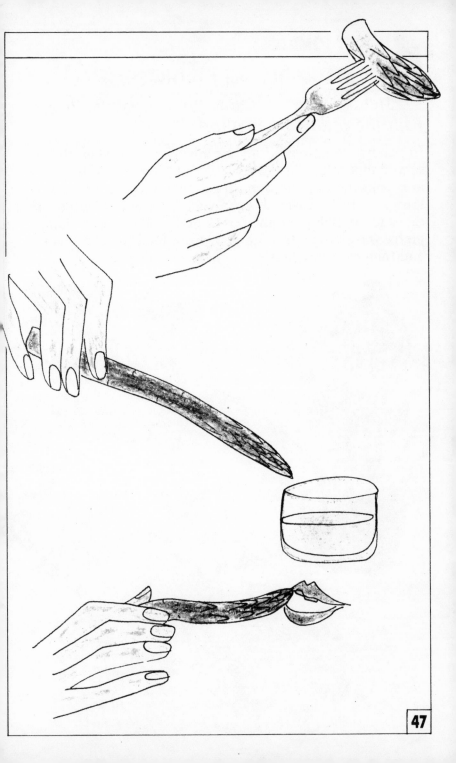

CHERRY TOMATOES

Cherry bombs can be devastating to fellow diners, unless you defuse them with the following methods.

Eat cherry tomatoes with your fingers except when they're served in a salad. Try to select small tomatoes to be put into your mouth, and don't try to bite into them because they will splurt. Instead, keep your lips firmly together. If there are only large tomatoes to be found on your plate, pierce the skin gently with your front teeth, bite off half, and then carefully finish.

CORN ON THE COB

With these kernels of knowledge, you'll really be able to get your teeth into corn!

Fresh corn on the cob will most likely be served at informal gatherings and can be broken in half to make it easier to handle. The key to eating it is not to butter or season too much at once. Going across or around the cob is a matter of personal choice; either method will work. Handle only a few rows or a section at once—buttering, salting, eating— and then repeat. This keeps the mess on your hands and face to a minimum.

SALAD

Take a leaf from the experts' book! You'll cut a wide swath through the greens with these easy-to-follow directions.

Salad is traditionally eaten with a fork. However, oversized pieces should be cut to avoid their springing off your fork. Historically, a steel knife stained black was used for salads and fruit, but stainless steel has changed the etiquette. A wedge of iceberg should always be eaten with a knife and fork. When the salad is served at the same time as your main course, don't transfer it onto your plate. If no salad plate is provided put it to the side of your main plate on your butter plate. A piece of bread or roll is often used against the fork to aid in pushing the salad onto it.

P OTATOES

No matter how you slice them, they can still make you feel thin-skinned.

Here are hints to toughen your resolve. Potato chips and shoestring potatoes are eaten with your fingers, unless the shoestrings are puddled in gravy, in which case you use a fork. Small French fries can be hand held but are preferably eaten with a fork. Cut them with your fork if they are too big to manage easily, and never dangle a large fry on your fork and nibble away at it. Ketchup is put on the side of your plate and the French fry is dipped into it, either by hand or a bite-size piece on a fork.

Baked potatoes are often already slit. If not, cut across the top with a knife, open wider with your fingers or a fork, and add butter or sour cream and chives, salt and pepper, a little at a time. You may eat the skin as you go along.

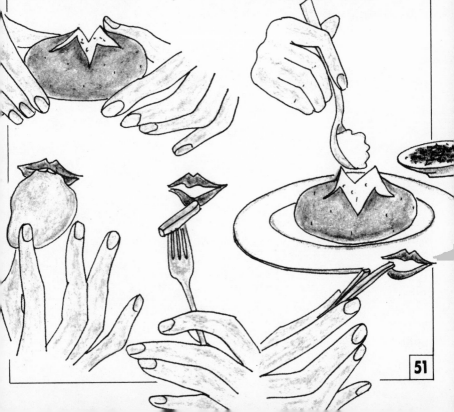

FINGER FOODS
*From Hand to Mouth
with Style and Security*

F INGER FOODS

Should you—or shouldn't you?

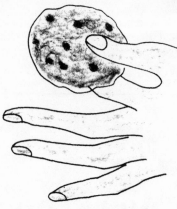

If you have any doubts, always follow your hostess's cue. And remember, when finger foods are on a platter, place them on your plate before you put them into your mouth. The following foods are meant to be eaten with the hands: corn on the cob, spareribs, clams and oysters on the half shell, lobster, sandwiches, dry cakes, cookies, some fruits (see each individual listing), crisp bacon, frogs' legs, chicken wings and bones in informal situations, shoestring potatoes or small French fries, and radishes, olives, and celery.

B|ACON

Bringing it home the gourmet way!

The rules are simply that bacon with any fat on it should be eaten with a knife and fork, but if it is very crisp, crumble it with a fork and eat it with your fingers.

B READ

Handling bread gracefully is the test of a well-bred diner,

but you can pass with flying colors as long as you remember to break slices of bread, rolls, and muffins in half or in small pieces before eating or buttering. Small biscuits do not have to be broken. Use your own butter knife and the butter on your plate; buttering should be done on the plate or just above it. Keep the butter knife slightly to the right with the handle off the edge to keep it clean.

Butter hot toast and muffins immediately. You don't have to break breadsticks. They can be buttered on one side. Cut Danish pastries (sweet rolls) into halves or quarters and butter each piece as you eat it.

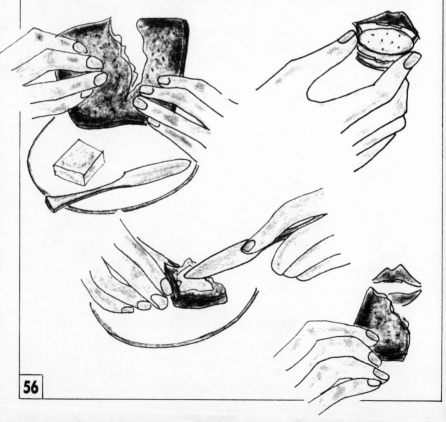

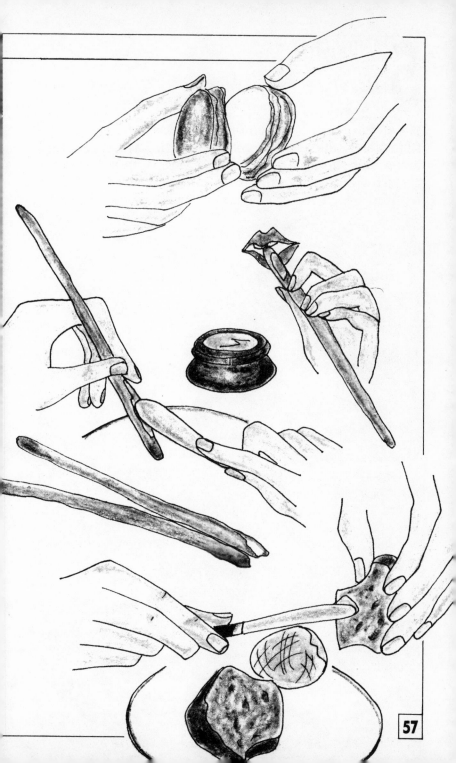

S ANDWICHES

Betwixt and between?

It's an easy decision if you always keep in mind that small sandwiches and canapés are eaten with fingers and that large ones should be cut before lifting. Any hot sandwich served with a gravy requires a knife and fork.

FORBIDDEN FRUITS
Or, Taming the Wild Mango

APPLES AND PEARS

No need to be thin-skinned about fruit etiquette—ever again!

At a dinner, an apple or pear is picked up with your hand and placed on your plate. If you can acquire the knack—it's a special talent—by all means peel in a spiral fashion. Since I'm not great at this, I place the piece on a dessert plate, halve it, core and cut it into smaller pieces, then eat it with a fork and a fruit knife. You can pick up the smaller pieces with your fingers if the meal situation is more informal.

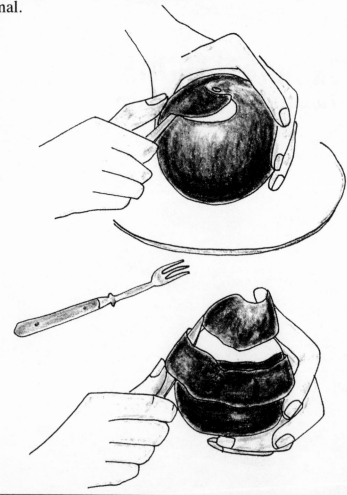

A VOCADO

Whether it's a strange fruit or a far-out vegetable, dispense with the guesswork and proceed with confidence.

An avocado served in its shell is eaten with a spoon and may come with salad dressing in the cavity; if it is sliced on a plate or in a salad, eat it with a fork.

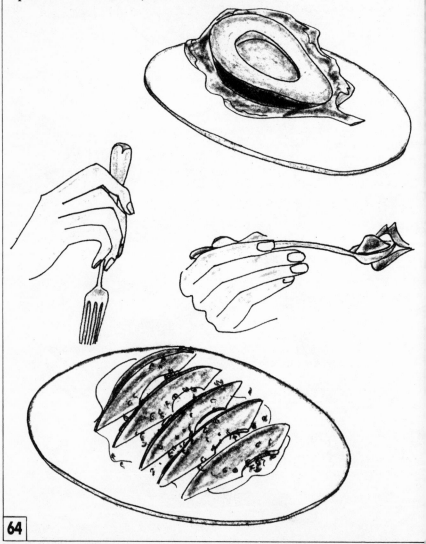

BANANA

You don't have to resort to monkey business!

If a banana is served at the dinner table, peel it, cut it with a (fruit) knife, and eat it with a fork. At all informal moments—picnics, the beach—eat it like a monkey.

BERRIES AND CHERRIES

Why pit yourself against them?

Go with the flow. Because there are so many ways to do this, you can take your pick. Eat berries with a spoon, whether they have cream on them or not.

Cherries are eaten by hand, the pits removed to your tightly cupped hand and deposited on your dessert plate.

G RAPES

No cause for sour grapes with these failproof tips!

Choose a branch and break it off, either with a scissors or by hand. Never pull off the grapes singly.

Seedless grapes are no problem; just eat them one by one. If they have seeds, place the grape in your mouth, chew, swallow the meat and allow any seeds to drop into your almost-closed fist.

To skin a grape easily, hold it stem-side against your mouth, squeeze it between your thumb and forefinger, and it will pop, pulp and juice, into your mouth. Leave the skins in your hand to put on your plate.

FIGS

It's not so hard to fig-ure out!

Fresh figs served as an appetizer with prosciutto are eaten skin and all with a knife and fork. If the little stem is still on the fig, cut it off (it's a tough chew if you don't!). As a dessert, quartered and drenched in orange juice or cream, they are eaten with a fork and spoon. Served *au naturel,* they are halved and eaten with a knife and fork.

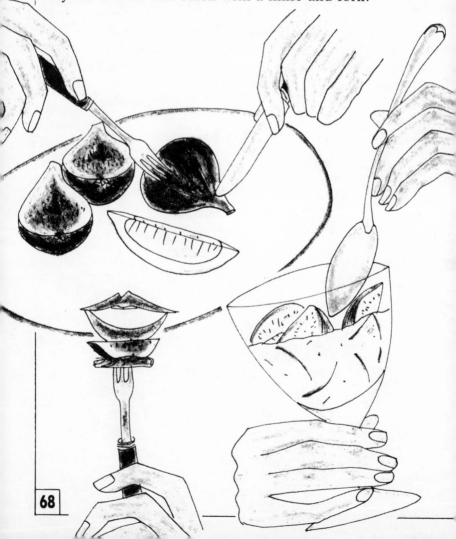

G RAPEFRUITS, ORANGES AND TANGERINES

Peel away the confusion, and you'll find simple solutions to your citrus quandaries.

Halved grapefruit is eaten with a teaspoon or a pointed grapefruit spoon. At informal meals, the juice can be carefully squeezed out onto the spoon.

GRAPEFRUITS, ORANGES AND TANGERINES

There are two ways to peel an orange; both begin with a sharp knife. Method one—a continuous spiral. The second method is to slice off the two ends and cut vertical stripes. Once peeled, sections can be pulled apart; if they are small, handle them from hand to mouth in one bite. If they are large, use a dessert fork and knife to cut and then eat. Oranges can also be eaten like grapefruit—halved with a grapefruit spoon or teaspoon, providing they've been pre-cut.

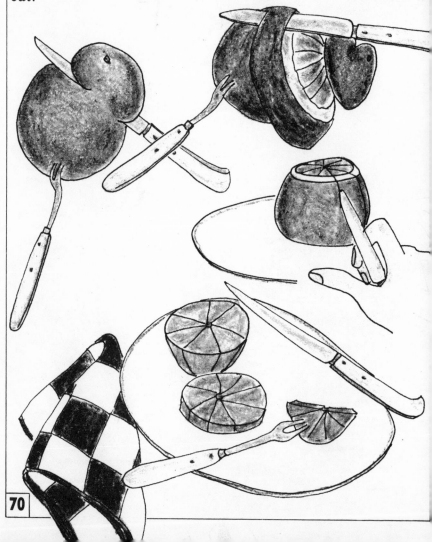

Tangerines are peeled by hand and eaten segment by
segment. You may want to peel the white pulpy covering,
if it is excessive.

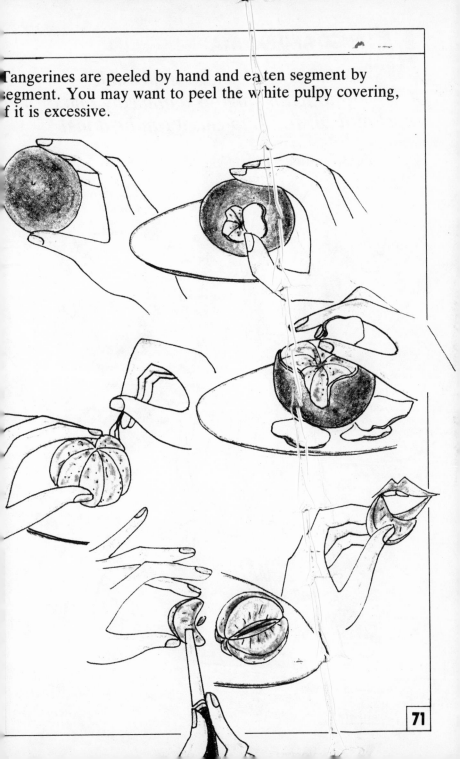

MANGO AND PAPAYA

Exotic doesn't mean impossible!
Although mango is admittedly one of the
most difficult fruits to eat, it can be done!

A whole mango should be cut in half with a sharp fruit knife, then cut into quarters, with the skin side up. Hold the mango down against your plate with a fork and pull the skin away. The mango can then be cut up and spoon-eaten. You may be served one that has been cut or at least halved with the stone removed, served in its skin, like an avocado and eaten with a spoon.

A papaya should be handled like an avocado or small melon that has been halved and its seeds scooped out; it is eaten with a spoon.

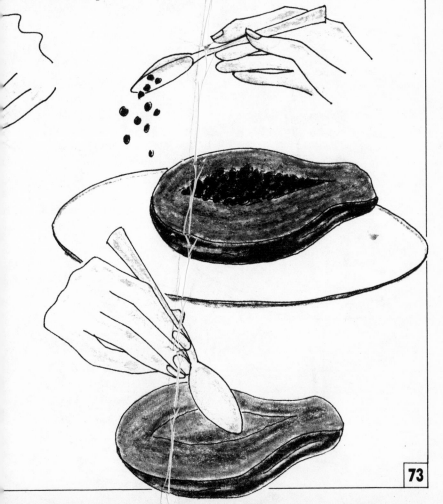

M ELON

How sweet it is to do it right!

Melon (honeydew, cantaloupe, casaba, or Persian) is eaten with a spoon. Only when it is skinned and served as a wedge is a fork used. The skinned wedge, accompanied by ham (prosciutto), is eaten with a knife and fork. If melon balls are served, with or without syrup, use a dessert spoon.

PEACHES

It's plum simple to eat a peach politely. Here's how.

Peaches or plums (nectarines, too) are halved, quartered and stoned with a knife. The skin can be pulled off, but it is perfectly acceptable to cut the fruit into smaller pieces with the skin on and eat it with a dessert fork and knife.

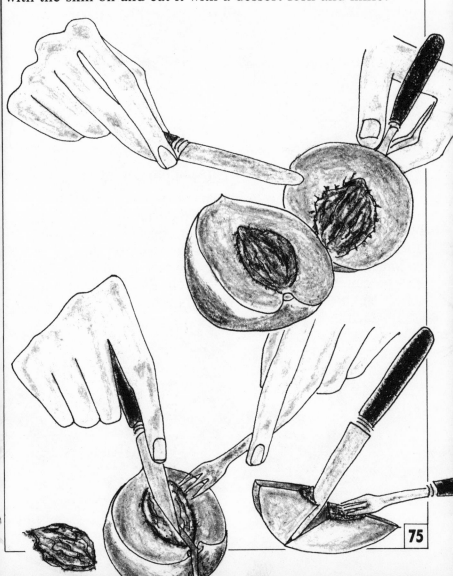

P ERSIMMON

Cutting through to table chic!

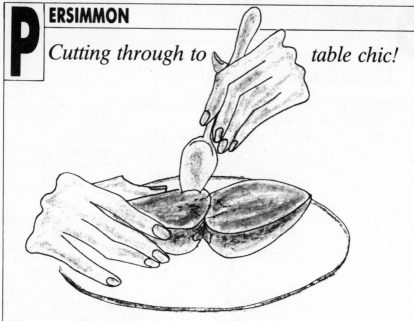

There are two ways to eat a persimmon.

One way is to cut it in half and scoop out the meat with a spoon. The second way is to set the fruit upright on the plate, stem end down, and cut it into quarters which are opened out until they lie flat. Cut each quarter into manageable pieces that can be eaten with a knife and fork. The pit can be cleaned in your mouth, then dropped onto a spoon and placed on the side of your plate. Never eat the skin, which tends to be bitter.

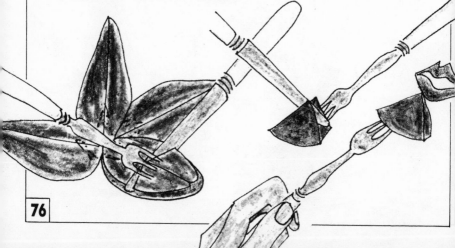

PINEAPPLE

Turn a tropical treasure into a dining room pleasure

by obeying this one simple rule: Always use a knife and fork to eat fresh pineapple slices.

STRAWBERRIES

Berry simple—if you know the secret!

Large strawberries may be eaten whole, grasped by the stem or dipped in powdered sugar (from one's own plate). Eat in a couple of bites and leave the stems on your plate.

If the strawberries are served in cream, use a spoon, of course.

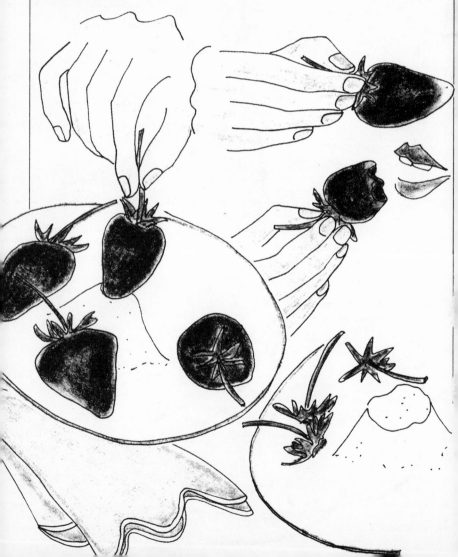

WATERMELON

If you've ever been stymied by what to do with the seeds (and who hasn't?), here's the answer to your problem.

Watermelon wedges are always eaten with a knife and fork. Any seeds taken into your mouth should be cleaned and dropped into your tightly cupped hand and put on your plate.

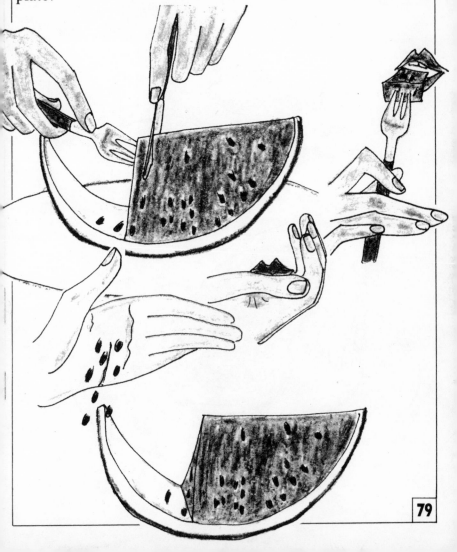

A seedy proposition? Not with the proper know-how!

Pomegranates are usually served in halves. Carefully extract a couple of the seeds on a spoon and eat them. You should secure the pomegranate half between your index finger and thumb while doing this.

ALIENS
Stuff Your Grandmother
Mostly Never Cooked

CRÊPES, BLINTZES AND TORTILLAS

Try as you might, you can't escape the crêpe.

There are almost as many kinds of crêpes as there are Frenchmen in Aisne, for every ethnic group has its own form of the stuffed pancake.

The dessert crêpe (crêpe suzette or blini) is eaten with a fork and spoon. Cutting and eating are done with the spoon—stabilizing with the fork.

The blintze, a thin pancake rolled around a cheese or fruit filling and either fried or baked, is eaten with a knife and fork. It is often accompanied by sour cream. A dollop of sour cream can be placed on each piece. Never dip a piece of blintze into the sour cream.

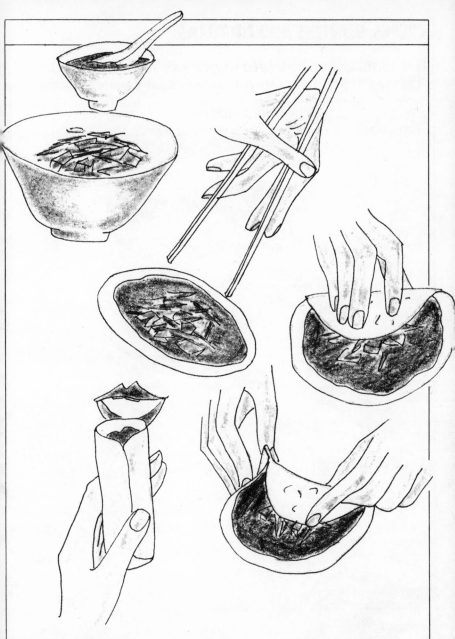

The Chinese crêpe may be filled with a mixture of meat (pork is typical), sauce and lettuce. It is rolled and eaten from the hand.

CRÊPES, BLINTZES AND TORTILLAS

Hot tortillas may be folded in quarters and buttered. Or you may hold one flat in your hand or on a plate, put some beans or other mixture in the center, and roll it like a cigar. Eat from one end to the other.

F ONDUE

Don't be afraid to plunge right in!

For cheese fondue, spear a piece of bread on a fondue fork
and dip it into the pot of hot cheese. Coat it, remove it
from the cheese, but hold it over the pot for a few seconds
to drip and cool—then eat. Try not to touch the fork with
your lips or tongue because it goes back into the pot.

FONDUE

For a meat fondue, plunge a speared piece of meat into the hot oil to cook. When it looks like it's done to your requirements, the meat is removed to a plate and eaten with a regular fork while your next piece is cooking. Accompanying the meat fondue is usually a choice of sauces; with either a ladle or serving spoon, put the sauces on your dinner plate. With your knife push some sauce onto your dinner fork that has speared the meat.

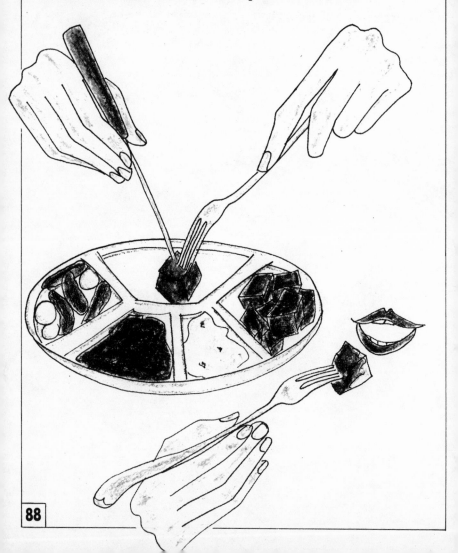

P ASTA

Basta pasta? Never! And here's your passport to gastronomic bliss.

Thick macaroni, lasagna or cannelloni can be cut with a fork if size requires it, and remaining sauce can be sopped up with fork-speared bread.

PASTA

Spaghetti is eaten with a fork. Pick up just a few strands and twirl them on fork. You may need the aid of a large spoon to help with the winding, but never lift the spoon from the plate. You can also have a small piece of bread in readiness to buttress the fork if you want to avoid the frowned-upon spoon. NEVER CUT SPAGHETTI.

If your platter comes with sauce and grated cheese on top of the pasta, it can be tossed with a spoon and a fork prior to eating. Any remaining sauce can be picked up with small pieces of speared bread.

PIZZA

If you're intimidated by devouring pizza in company, remember that in Italy even the children can do it!

A pie-shaped wedge of pizza is held in your fingers with the sides curled up to avoid losing the filling. If the slice is large, you may eat it with a knife and fork.

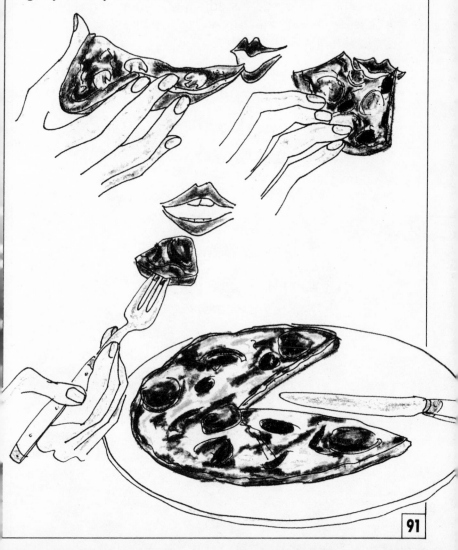

SWEET SOMETHINGS
Getting Your Just Desserts

C AKE AND PASTRY

*Eating a piece of cake should be . . .
a piece of cake.*

Usually it's eaten with a fork, but if you are offered a fruit tart with a dessert spoon and fork, secure the tart with the fork and cut with the spoon; then eat it with the spoon.

Pie is eaten with a fork unless it's *à la mode,* in which case both a fork and spoon are used.

If you are offered a creamy pastry such as a Napoleon or cream puff, it's advisable to use a fork rather than your hand, in order to keep the good stuff from oozing out the other end.

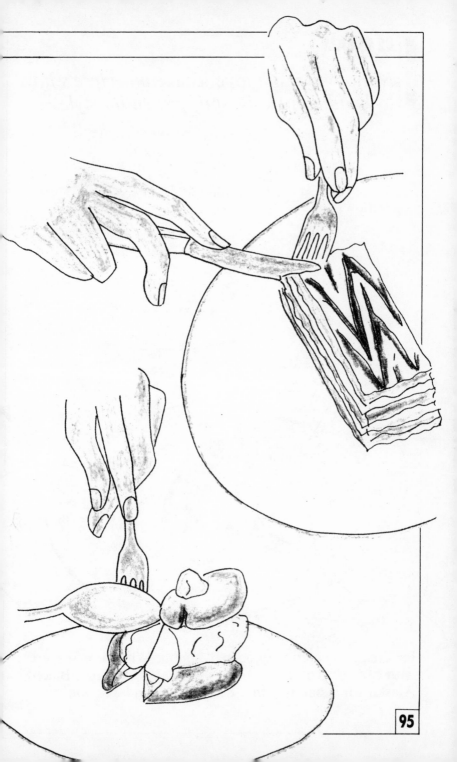

CE CREAM

Nobody doesn't love ice cream. Here's how to handle the kids' stuff grown-up style.

Ice cream is eaten with a small spoon. When it is served with cake or pie or as part of a dish (for example, Baked Alaska), it is eaten with a dessert fork and a spoon.

P | LUM PUDDING

Though it doesn't contain plums and isn't really a pudding, this traditional dessert is certain to challenge you at holiday time. You can meet it with aplomb by keeping in mind a few principles!

After the brandy with which the pudding is flamed dies down, it is usually served in a dessert bowl, often accompanied by a bowl of ice cream or sauce. Either of these or both are scooped onto your pudding—all to be eaten with a spoon. If brandy is passed at this moment, pour some onto your pudding—not into your glass.

POACHED PEARS

Trickier to manage than you might assume, this divine dessert is worth the trouble.

Eat with a spoon and a fork. The fork holds the pear down against the dish and the spoon is used to cut the fruit into small edible pieces. The fork can be used to rotate the fruit around to get at all the flesh. If only a spoon is provided, use your hand to rotate the dish. Leave the core in the dish and spoon out the wine or syrup.

S HERBET

The quintessential palate cleanser at many points in a meal, sherbet is refreshingly simple to deal with.

When it is served as an accompaniment to a meat course or with a fruit cup, it may be eaten with a fork. If it is served as a dessert, use a spoon.

STEWED FRUIT

Compote yourself with class!

Stewed fruit is eaten with a spoon, but you may want to resort to a fork to steady some of the larger pieces. All pits from cherries, prunes, plums are to be deposited from your mouth onto the spoon and onto the side of your plate.

ADDENDA
Effortless Extras That Add a Lot of Style

BUTTER

To smear or not to smear? That is the question. Now, here are the answers.

To butter breads, rolls, biscuits, or toast, use a knife and small pieces of butter on small pieces of bread. Do not butter vegetables, because it's an insult to the cook. (See listings for corn on the cob and potatoes for special instructions.)

C ONDIMENTS

Learning to take the bitter with the sweet.

Horseradish, mint jelly, currant jelly, mustard, apple butter, cranberry sauce are spooned onto the plate next to the meat or fowl. You incorporate them onto your fork with a bit of the meat or fowl.

Liquid sauces, such as mint, cherry sauce or apricot duck sauce, are to be poured judiciously right onto the meat. A small amount is preferable, so that you don't overwhelm the taste of the meat.

Jellies, jams and conserves for rolls and biscuits are to be spooned onto the side of your butter plate and spread on small pieces of the bread or roll with a knife. If a spoon isn't available for serving, wipe your knife on the edge of the plate before touching the jelly in the serving jar or bowl.

For curried dishes, condiments, such as peanuts, coconut and chutney, can be spooned onto your plate and tossed with the curry. Chutney has the option of being eaten as an accompaniment.

G ARNISHES

Serve them with style, then eat them with relish!

When relishes (celery, olives, radishes, etc.) are passed to you from a tray, either use a serving spoon, if it is provided, or serve them onto your butter plate, or your main dish if there is no butter dish. Never put them directly into your mouth. If you want to salt them, shake some salt on the plate next to them and, using your fingers, dip and eat. Olives are taken whole into the mouth and pits are removed to a tightly cupped fist and put on your butter plate.

Pickles are eaten with your fingers when they accompany a sandwich. When served with meat they are eaten with a knife and fork.

Dill, parsley and watercress are eaten with a fork as part of the meal. They may be eaten with fingers—but never when they are covered with salad dressing or sauce.

Thin lemon slices are decoration. Lemon wedges or halves are meant to be squeezed. Gently pierce the pulp with a fork, squeeze over the food to be seasoned with one hand while the other hand shields the lemon to prevent squirting. Some restaurants cover lemon halves with cheesecloth to avoid squirting.

A light touch is the key!

Gravy or sauce should never be poured or ladled onto everything on your plate at random, but exclusively on the dish it was intended for. If you wish to "sop up" the extra gravy (and it is a compliment to the cook to do so), put down a small piece of bread into the sauce and retrieve it with your fork—tines down. One small piece of bread at a time.

HONEY

*A sticky situation can develop,
but it needn't.*

To handle honey, all you do is to twist it onto the spoon—
the thinner the honey, the more rapid the motion—and
then drop it onto the butter plate.

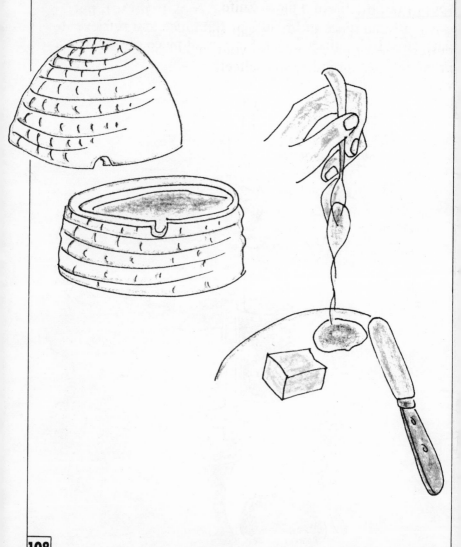

SALT AND PEPPER

You don't have to be a grind to learn to do it right.

Add salt and pepper only after you taste the food. It is an insult to do so before. If there is a saltcellar, a small open bowl of salt, use the spoon that's in it; if there isn't a spoon, use the tip of a clean knife.

Anything to be dipped in salt should be put on your butter plate or on the edge of your dinner plate. If you are provided with an individual saltcellar, you can take a pinch with your fingers.

CHIC TECHNIQUES
How to Pass as a Seasoned Gourmet—Instantly

WHICH SILVER TO USE FIRST

Thou shalt not covet thy neighbor's knife—and you'll never be accused of it if you obey these culinary commandments.

The general rule is to start from the outside and work your way toward the plate. Dessert fork and spoon are usually supplied as needed or sometimes are placed at the top of the plate, horizontal to the table edge.

There are two styles for cutting: the two-step European or Continental style and the four-step crossover American style. Both are acceptable.

In the two-step cutting method, the knife is held in the right hand and the fork in the left throughout the procedure. With the tines of the fork facing down, the food is cut and the fork brought to the mouth, tines down.

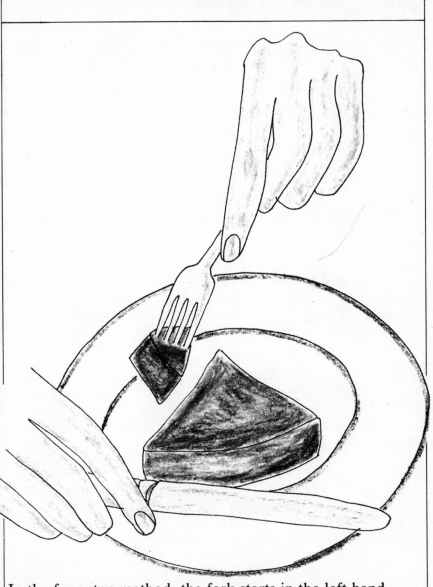

In the four-step method, the fork starts in the left hand, the knife in the right, and the main dish is cut. The knife is placed flat on the plate and the fork is switched to the free right hand and turned right side up in the process. It is brought to the mouth in the right hand.

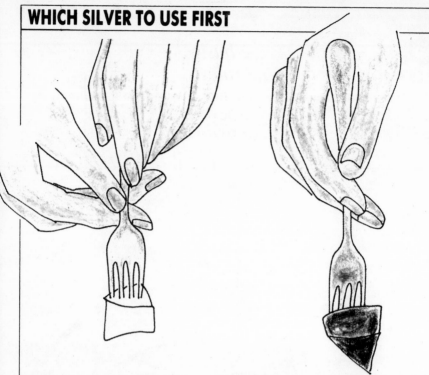

When resting between bites, place the knife and fork, handles to the right, on the plate. Never rest them on the table. When you're finished, place the silver side by side, across the middle of the plate, handles right, to secure its removal.

Food is always served from the left, and the silver service fork is placed to the left of the spoon and both are angled in toward the food so they can be easily picked up by the next person served. And start eating *hot* food when it is served—do not wait for everyone to begin.

FORMAL SETTINGS

Once you learn the basics, it's smooth sailing because the rules never change.

This is an example of a formal five-course meal—soup, fish, meat, salad and three wines. Dessert service will be presented at the end of these courses.

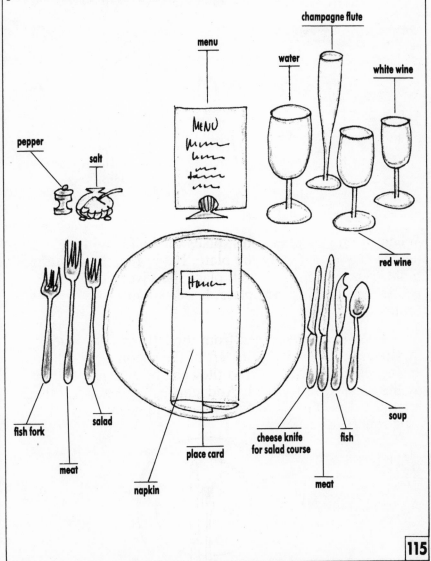

champagne flute

water

white wine

menu

pepper

salt

red wine

fish fork

salad

meat

napkin

place card

cheese knife
for salad course

fish

meat

soup

Setting the scene . . .

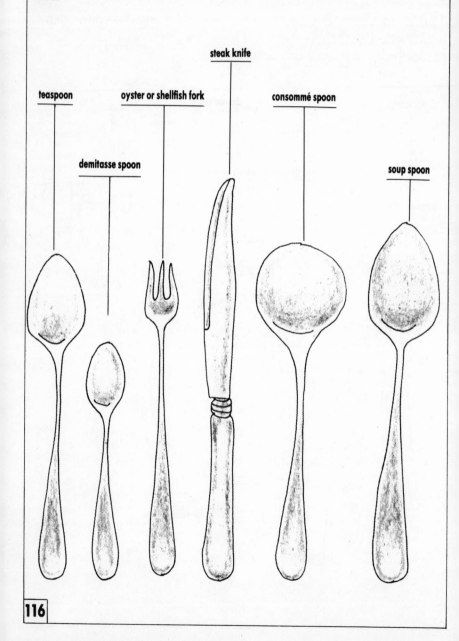

teaspoon

demitasse spoon

oyster or shellfish fork

steak knife

consommé spoon

soup spoon

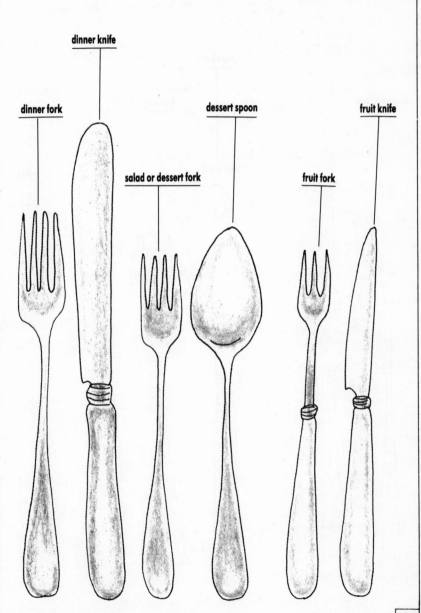

dinner fork

dinner knife

salad or dessert fork

dessert spoon

fruit fork

fruit knife

EATING UTENSILS IDENTIFIED

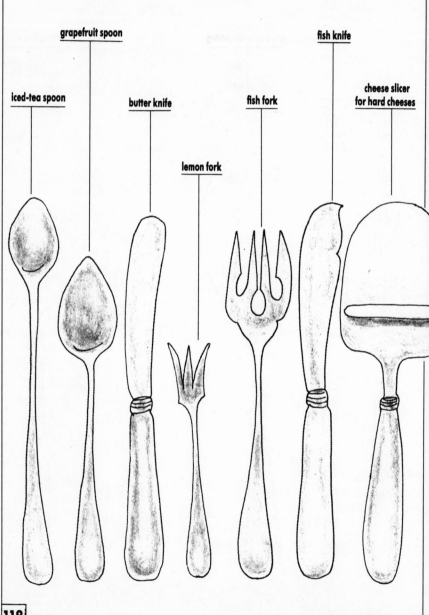

iced-tea spoon

grapefruit spoon

butter knife

lemon fork

fish fork

fish knife

cheese slicer
for hard cheeses

salad spoon for serving

salad fork for serving

serving fork

serving spoon

P APER WRAPPERS

If you've ever been torn between the ashtray and the floor, here's what you should really do with those little pieces of paper.

Sugar wrappers can be tucked under your saucer or next to your plate, lying flat. Leave butter wrappers or jelly containers on your butter plate.

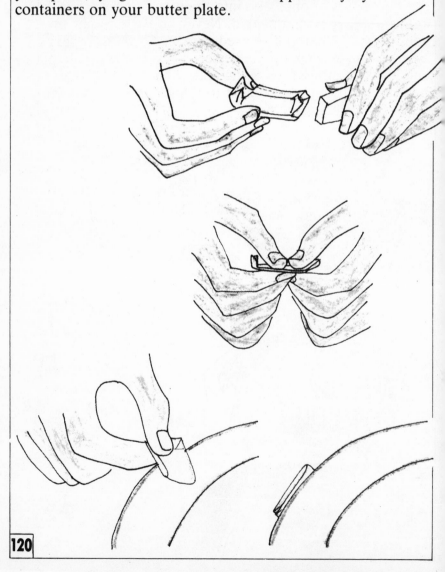

FINGER BOWLS

Afraid of looking dippy when a finger bowl appears? Just cool it!

Finger bowls are genuinely helpful after eating artichokes, shellfish, corn on the cob, asparagus or any other hand-held food. And they're easier to use than you might think. Just dip the fingers of one hand into the bowl, then the other, and wipe them with a napkin. Never bring the water to your mouth. After you've used a finger bowl, presented on a dessert plate, pick up the dessert silver if it is on the plate and put it to either side of the plate, then lift the finger bowl and its doily and place it to the left of the plate. This requires two hands.

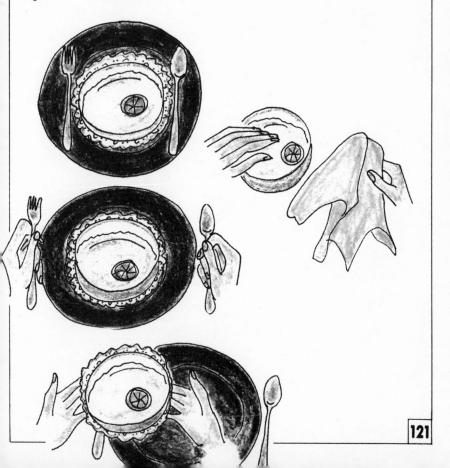

N APKINS

The lap of luxury is only four steps away!

A large dinner napkin is placed on the lap folded halfway. If it is a luncheon-sized napkin, open it all the way. If you leave a table during a meal and at its conclusion, never put your napkin on a chair. Always place it loosely folded to either the right or left of your plate.

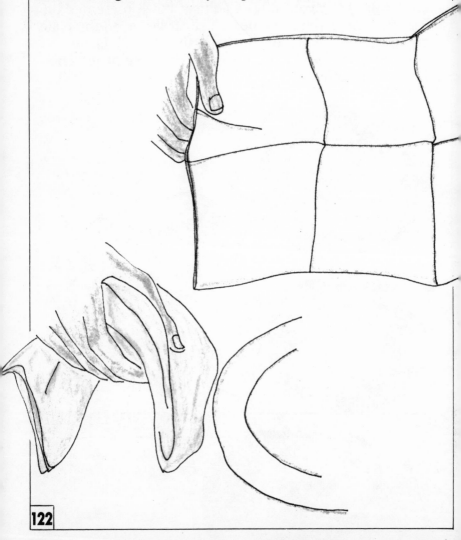

HOW TO USE CHOPSTICKS

There's an art to this all right, but you don't have to be an inscrutable Oriental to get the knack.

Pick up one chopstick as you would a pencil, in the middle of the chopstick between the base of your thumb and your index finger, using your third and fourth fingers for support. This leaves your index finger free. Place the second chopstick parallel to the first, holding it firmly between the thumb and index finger. The first chopstick remains firm while the second one is used as a lever. Lift the small bowls of rice to just below your mouth for eating—rather than lowering head to plate. Place the chopsticks across the bowl or plate between bites or at the end of the meal. Some Japanese restaurants provide a small ceramic piece to rest chopsticks on.

Do not be embarrassed to ask for help, and if you are more comfortable using a fork, ask for one.

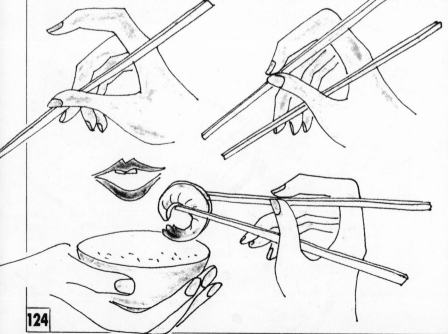

HOW TO DRINK IT

From the first glass to the last mug, here's how to deal with mealtime beverages like a pro.

Drinking from a mug is usual today in informal settings. A saucer may be provided underneath for you to put your teaspoon on. Most often there isn't one. If there are paper mats, the spoon may be placed face down onto it, or on the edge of a butter plate or dinner plate. Don't drink from a mug with a spoon in it. You run the risk of poking out your eyes.

Teabags should be placed against the edge of your saucer after the excess liquid has been squeezed out of them either by pressing the bag against the side of your cup or mug with your spoon, or setting the bag in the spoon and wrapping the string around the bowl of the spoon and bag, then squeezing. If there isn't a saucer or plate, ask for one. Remove long-handled spoons from iced tea or coffee before drinking.

HOW TO DRINK IT

If coffee or tea slops into your saucer ask for a new saucer.
If this is inconvenient to do and paper napkins are
available, use one to absorb the liquid on the saucer and let
it sit there as a sponge. This is more advantageous than
dripping across a table, cloth cover or yourself.

A red wine glass is held at the base of the bowl. A glass of
white wine is held by the stem—to preserve its chill.

A brandy snifter is warmed in both hands by rolling the
bowl between your hands and then cupped in one hand.
The warming brings out the bouquet.

If there are olives, onions or cherries in your drink, you may remove them with your fingers; it is easier to wait until all the liquid is drunk, when you can tip the glass back to allow the "garnish" to slip into your mouth.

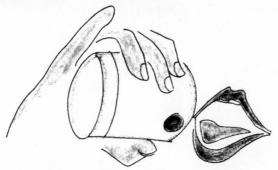

Never put a glass down on an unprotected surface in someone's house. Ask for a coaster.

If you spill liquid, try not to create too much of a fuss. Simply ask the host or hostess where you can find a cloth or sponge to clean it up.

Never "dunk" anything into your drink.

Don't ever blow on a hot drink to cool it. Stir it quietly and/or wait it out until it cools.